Thomas A. Edison

The World's Greatest Inventor

Anna Sproule

BLACKBIRCH PRESS, INC.

WOODBRIDGE, CONNECTICUT

Published by Blackbirch Press, Inc.
260 Amity Road
Woodbridge, CT 06525
web site: http://www.blackbirch.com
e-mail: staff@blackbirch.com

First published in Great Britain as *Scientists Who Have Changed the World* by Exley Publications Ltd., Chalk Hill, Watford, 1991.
© Exley Publications, Ltd., 1990

10 9 8 7 6 5 4 3

Photo Credits:
Cover: Courtesy of U.S. Department of the Interior/NPS; Ann Ronan: 6, 24, 36, 48; Nick Birch: 12, 13, 26, 29, 34-35, 38, 46 (both); The Bridgeman Art Library: 12-13, 16, 18, 22, 42, 43; Paul Brierley: 58; British Museum: 4; The Cincinnati Historical Society: 18; The Edison National Historic Site: 23, 27, 32, 45, 56; Mary Evans: 10, 21, 30-31 (all), 55; Michael Holford: 19; Angelo Hornak: 40; Mansell Collection: 14; The New York Historical Society: 28; Science Photo Library: 39, 59; Wayland Picture Library: 53; Zefa: 8-9, 17, 50.

Printed in China

Library of Congress Cataloging-in-Publication Data
Sproule, Anna.
  Thomas A. Edison : the world's greatest inventor / by Anna Sproule — 1st U.S. ed.
    p. cm.—(Giants of science)
  Includes bibliographical references and index.
  Summary: Details the life and work of Thomas Edison, who developed the electric light bulb and patents for numerous other inventions and innovations.
  ISBN 1-56711-331-1 (hardcover : alk. paper)
  1. Edison, Thomas A. (Thomas Alva), 1847-1931—Juvenile literature. 2. Inventors—United States—Biography—Juvenile literature. [1. Edison, Thomas A. (Thomas Alva), 1847-1931. 2. Inventors.] I. Title. II. Series.
TK140 .E3 S67 2000   00-008072
621.3'092—dc21   CIP
                      AC

Contents

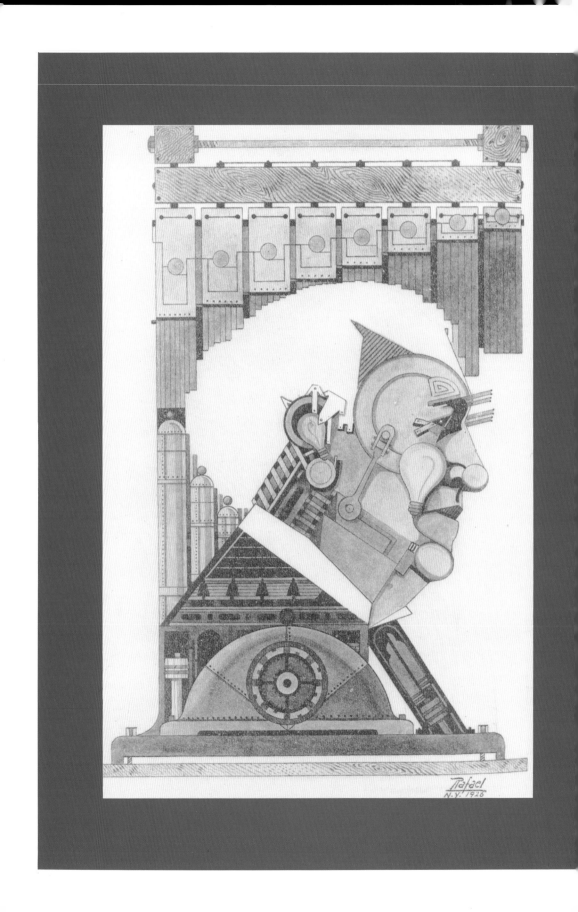

The Sound of the Past

The machine talked. All but one of the men who stood around it that December evening in 1877 felt a chill run down their backs. Outside the laboratory, the fields and lanes of the New Jersey landscape were gripped by the coming winter. It wasn't the cold wind or the approach of winter, though, that made the lab workers shiver.

No human being had ever heard a noise like the one that the little machine produced. The men were listening to the sound of someone talking. It wasn't actually someone talking to them right then. It was someone talking to them from the past. They were hearing the first recording of a human voice ever made.

The first words retrieved from the past did not quite convey the importance of the moment. Crackling but distinct, the voice on the machine recited a fragment of a nursery rhyme:

"Mary had a little lamb,
Its fleece was white as snow,
And everywhere that Mary went
The lamb was sure to go . . ."

There was a stunned silence. "God in Heaven," breathed John Kreusi, the bushy-bearded Swiss watchmaker who had made the machine's bright brass cylinder and the handle that turned it. Abruptly, the silence ended. The men laughed, slapped one another's backs, and shouted with joy.

Opposite: *This portrait by a South American artist portrays Thomas A. Edison as a man made by technology.*

5

This sketch was made at a Paris exhibition where its inventor was know as the "astonishing Edison."

The Man Who Could Not Hear

The only person who didn't join in the laughter was the machine's inventor, Thomas Edison. He was the lab's owner and boss, known by his staff as the "Old Man." Deaf from boyhood, Edison heard only silence. Although he could hear nothing, he knew why the rest of the crew was laughing enough to bring the roof down. Edison could see their positive reaction to what had happened.

As he pushed his tousled hair back off his forehead, the inventor bent over the table, re-adjusted the machine, and turned the handle again. Obediently, the cylinder with its tinfoil cover turned, moving along the rod on which it was mounted. As it went along, the cylinder moved under a blunt needle, mounted at the end of a short, stubby tube. And, from the other end of the tube, came the familiar words again, "Mary had a little lamb . . ."

Though the sound crackled and was scratchy, this time the "Old Man" managed to hear it. It was Edison's own voice, captured a few minutes before as he had recited the nursery rhyme. The process by which the recording was made and played was rather simple. One needle on the far side of the cylinder had changed the sound into a groove that was etched in the tinfoil. The groove wound round and round the cylinder from one end to another. As the cylinder turned, the playing needle was now running over the same groove its twin had scratched. And, as it ran, it played the rhyme back to the exulting audience. It was all so simple. Awed, the inventor stared at his invention.

With "Mary Had a Little Lamb," the world's sound recording industry had been born. Called the phonograph, or "sound writer," the machine with the revolving cylinder was the ancestor of the gramophone, the record player, and the compact disc. Its creator was also the world's first recording artist. He was Thomas Alva Edison, aged thirty, a rumpled, self-taught inventor who still spoke with the nasal twang of the American Midwest where he had been born.

A Whole New World

Thomas Edison was perhaps one of the greatest inventors who has ever lived. He did not merely change the world he was living in. His inventions helped to bring a totally different world into

"We are inclined to regard him as one of the wonders of the world."

"Scientific American," commenting on Edison and the phonograph, 1878

Edison helped to create the modern world, such as present-day New York with its millions of lights.

existence—the one we are living in today. The phonograph was only one of his incredible creations. Another was the first successful movie camera, along with the equipment for viewing films. Edison also transformed the early telephone invented by Alexander Graham Bell and made it work better. He did the same with the typewriter. He also worked on projects as varied as vacuum-packing food, and building houses cheaply out of concrete. Above all, he helped to bring civilization out of the Age of Steam into the Age of Electricity.

If you look at an electric lightbulb, you will see a reminder of Edison's greatest achievement. He created the threadlike filament that glows when the light is turned on. Other inventors had worked

on similar experiments. In Britain, the great scientist Joseph Swan had made his breakthrough at almost the same time that Edison did. But Edison had taken his work much further.

Without electricity, the lightbulb was of no use. So he created an entire system—from the great dynamos that produce electric power to the sockets on lightbulbs themselves.

The Skeptics Were Wrong

Plenty of people scoffed at Edison's ideas. There was only one way of getting back at all the skeptics: hours, days, weeks—even years trying one experiment after another until something worked.

Despite his lack of schooling, Edison made

things work. People now believe that this igno-rance actually helped him to work things out. The self-taught inventor, who left school when he was only twelve, didn't believe that anything was impossible. He just barged ahead and proved the doubters wrong.

A Risky Birth

Thomas Alva Edison was born before dawn on February 11, 1847, in the snow-swept town of Milan, Ohio, near Lake Erie. His parents were Canadians. His father owned a timber business. His mother, almost forty at the time of his birth, already had six children, and had seen three of them die. When Nancy Edison's seventh baby was born, she feared that he might die, too. He was weak, and his head looked too big. Despite Nancy's fears, the newest Edison survived. His parents gave him the family name of Thomas. His father, Sam, decided to honor a business friend by giving baby Tom the middle name of Alva. Shortened to "Al," it became the name he was called as a child.

Full of Curiosity

Young Al was sometimes lonely. His brother and two sisters were much older than he was and they no longer lived at home.

But young Al soon discovered that there was plenty to play with. His little town was full of excitement. There was his father's timber yard, with its nose-tingling smells. There was the canal to swim in (where Al nearly drowned). There was the big flour mill, full of steam-driven machinery. Even better, there was the mill's owner, who was building a balloon to take people into the air!

Full of curiosity, Al had his nose into everything. He'd watch, wonder, and bombard people with questions. Then, armed with possible answers,

Opposite: *Edison lounges against a bench in the laboratory he built in the New Jersey countryside.*

11

Edison was twelve when he left school to earn his living as a newspaper boy.

he'd test out his new-found knowledge for himself. Once, young Al asked his mother why a goose sat on her eggs. His mother told him. Al then wanted to know why the goose wanted to keep her eggs warm. His mother told him that, too. Soon afterwards, he vanished for the afternoon. When his father found him, Al was asleep in the barn. Underneath him, in a mass of cracked shells and leaking yolks, was a collection of fresh farmyard eggs. Geese, he realized, could hatch eggs—but people couldn't!

Bottom of the Class

Al loved learning things for himself. But school was different. Imprisoned every day in one room, he felt utterly lost.

Like most teachers of the time, the schoolmaster

believed in using a cane to beat knowledge into his pupils. Even though the beatings frightened Al, he still couldn't learn the long lists of facts that his teacher assigned. His habit of asking questions only made the teacher more angry. Al couldn't always hear what the teacher said. Because he was bored, he always got into trouble.

Al sank to the bottom of the class and stayed there for three months. One day the schoolmaster described Young Edison as "addled." In a rage, the young boy rushed out of the schoolroom and refused to go back.

Education at Home

At home, Al's mother took his side by letting him run his own education. Most of the time, she taught Al herself. With her encouragement, he

Above left: *Covered wagons heading west were a frequent sight in Al's birthplace of Milan, Ohio. This small midwestern town was sketched around the time that Edison lived in one.*

Above right: *The room where Thomas Alva Edison was born.*

13

As a boy, Edison watched a hot-air balloon being built by Milan's miller, Sam Winchester. Without knowing it, Winchester taught Al about scientific persistence.

read Shakespeare, history books, and the Bible. Sensing his interest, Al's mother also gave him a book on science. Called the *School of Natural Philosophy*, it was full of simple experiments that Al could do at home. From that moment, his life was transformed.

Al quickly read the entire book and did all the experiments. Then he made up his own. He bought chemicals, scrounged supplies, and set up a laboratory in his bedroom. In one of his experiments, Al attempted to create static electricity by rubbing together the fur of two big cats, whose tails he had attached to wires. The only result was that he got scratched and clawed!

Al's mother gave her son her blessing—up to a point. Angry over her wrecked furniture, Mrs. Edison insisted that the lab be moved down to the basement. Thuds and explosions sometimes shook the house. They startled Al's father who, like the schoolmaster, was always ready to use the cane on his preoccupied, headstrong son. But Nancy would calm Sam down by telling him that their son knew quite well what he was doing.

The Newsboy

The year 1859 was an important year for the people of Port Huron. The railway came, linking the lakeside town with the bustling city of Detroit.

Before the railway, North America was full of small, isolated towns that had little or no contact or communication between them. The only means of transportation for both goods and people was by horse-drawn carriage—across thousands of miles of wild territory.

Twelve-year-old Al decided to get a job on the new railway. He had several reasons. His family was short of money, and he always needed cash for his expensive hobby.

With his father's help, Al got a job as a newsboy on the train on the Port Huron-Detroit line. Besides newspapers, Al sold candy and refreshments. Carrying baskets of wares, Al would walk up and down between the seats, shouting, "Peanuts, popcorn, chewing gum, candy!"

Trains and Chemicals

Al's day started at dawn, when he got up to catch the morning train south to Detroit. The evening train to Port Huron got back at half past nine. Then the newsboy still had to get home, in a horse-drawn cart that he drove himself.

Al was gloriously happy. He was now making money. During the day he could spend his free time reading at the Detroit Public Library. The guards let him keep his candy and newspapers in an empty luggage van. Gradually, Al installed his chemicals and equipment there, too. All went well until one of his experiments started a fire. The guard, who got burned, threw the whole laboratory out onto the tracks!

The Battle of Shiloh

Al was still working on the Detroit-Port Huron train when the Civil War broke out in 1861. For four years the northern and southern states fought each other over issues such as the abolition of slavery. One dreadful battle followed another, and the public became desperate for news. Al found it difficult to estimate how many papers he would sell on any particular day. If he had too few, he lost business. If he had too many, he lost money. To get around this problem, Al made sure he saw an advance copy of the newspaper's main story before he caught the morning train. That way he could be sure he had plenty of newspapers on days when the news was important.

> "The happiest time in my life was when I was twelve years old. I was just old enough to have a good time in the world, but not old enough to understand any of its troubles."
>
> Thomas Edison in 1930, recalling his boyhood

On April 6, 1862, some important news came into the Detroit newspaper office. There had been a major battle in a place called Shiloh. Over 20,000 men were lying dead or injured. For anyone in the newspaper business, this was a very big story. If only, thought paperboy Al, the news of the battle of Shiloh could be sent to all the towns along the Detroit-Port Huron line. He'd sell hundreds of papers. Suddenly, Al realized that he could make it happen. He could send a message to Detroit using electricity. He would use the telegraph.

The Electric Telegraph

In 1862, the main job of electricity was sending messages over long distances by using the telegraph, a system referred to as the "long-distance writer." Before the telegraph, people communicated over long distances by using signaling methods

Civil War river battles were fought with ironclad ships.

such as semaphore, but these generally only worked if the signalers were close enough to see each other. And even if they were, signals in bad weather or after dark were almost impossible to read. The electric telegraph, on the other hand, could carry messages much further.

A special piece of equipment, called an electromagnet, made the telegraph work. It had been invented forty years earlier. It was a piece of metal with a length of wire coiled around it. As the current traveled along the wire, the metal became a magnet, attracting iron. The effect only lasted as long as the current flowed through the wire. To work the telegraph, an operator at one end of the line tapped a lever. This sent a jolt of electric current flowing down the wire. At the other end, the current turned a piece of metal into an electromagnet. The wire attracted an iron lever that had a pencil fixed to it.

A survey team responsible for mapping out the geography of Wyoming takes a supper break. Communication by telegraph made westward expansion possible in the late 1800s.

Once the current activated the electromagnet, the lever caused the pencil to make a mark on a roll of paper as it moved.

Short Taps and Long Taps

Samuel Morse, the man who designed the American telegraph, also invented the code that the pencil used. A short tap on the key at one end of the line made the pencil at the other end write a dot. A firmer, longer tap made a dash. Each letter of the alphabet had its own dot-and-dash code. Operators at the other end of the wire read the rows of dots and dashes and turned them back into ordinary writing.

It was a simple system that had become even simpler by Edison's time. Experienced operators recognized the pattern of short and long clicks so quickly that could decode messages straight off the machine.

Al could decode messages himself, but very slowly. The year before, in 1860, he had set up his own homemade telegraph that he operated between his home and that of a friend. He powered it with batteries from his basement. On the day of

Opposite top: *Young Edison spent several years of his life drifting as a "tramp" telegrapher riding on trains like this one.*

Opposite bottom: *The battle of Shiloh was one of the bloodiest battles of the Civil War.*

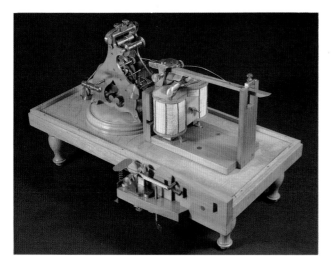

Left: *A telegraph from Edison's time.*

the battle of Shiloh, he knew he needed the help of a professional. He needed the telegraph operator at the Detroit Station.

Read All About It!

Al raced down to the Detroit Station and begged the telegraph operator to contact all the stations down the line. He wanted to tell them that a great battle had taken place at Shiloh. In return, he promised the operator a free subscription to not one but two magazines—and he would throw in a free newspaper each day for six months!

Usually, Al bought 100 papers to sell to his customers. This time, he asked for 1,500! As the train rumbled out of Detroit, Al could scarcely wait to get the newspapers and find out if the telegrapher had kept his word and sent the story by Morse code.

The telegrapher had! The headline story was about Shiloh. Usually, Al only sold 2 papers at the first station on the line. With the battle on the front page, Al sold 200 newspapers. At the next station, he sold 300—and raised the price of the newspaper! By the time Al reached Port Huron, the price had reached a quarter of a dollar and was still rising. By the end of the day, young Al had made a magnificent profit.

Perfecting the Telegraph

No one was surprised when, at age sixteen, Al became a telegraph operator himself. After Shiloh, he began to study telegraphy with an operator on his train route, using the transmitting key and working on his speed at receiving messages. Al's first job was in the telegraph office in Port Huron, his hometown. Not many messages came to Port Huron, so there was plenty of time to experiment with the batteries, wires, and other electrical equipment lying around the office. It was almost as good as his old

The telegraph was not the only method of long-distance communication used by Americans in the late 1800s. This engraving shows an alternative system of sending signals.

lab on the train. His lab at the telegraph office ended in much the same way, however. While he was conducting one of his experiments, Al almost blew the office up! It was time to move on.

For the next five years, young Edison wandered the United States and the nearby border areas of Canada, working as a "tramp" telegrapher.

Al's skills as a telegraph receiver grew all the time. But so did his hearing troubles. Still in his teens, Al was becoming deaf. Oddly enough, his deafness actually helped him in his work. The sharp clicking of the telegraph machine came clearly through the muffled sounds that filled his ears.

Al was good at his work, and he knew it. He played jokes, made up messages, and went on with his experiments—on the job and after hours.

Experiments—and Getting Fired

Al's bosses liked his scientific tinkering even less than they liked his cockiness. After he left Port

In the 1870s, Al produced a "multiplex" system that allowed several messages to travel over a wire at the same time. In this sketch, four messages are passing along the same wire.

Huron, he moved to Stratford, Ontario, where he worked the night shift. Al preferred working nights because it left the days free for science. To show they were awake, night workers had to send a special signal to headquarters every so often. This did not please Al because he had better things to do. So he rigged up a clock with a timer that sent the signal down the wire automatically every hour!

One place fired Al because he spilled a jar of acid during an experiment. The acid burned through the floor, the ceiling below, and the carpet of the room downstairs. The firings, however, weren't always for a good reason. In Memphis, Tennessee, Al used a repeater, another telegraph gadget he'd invented to set up a direct link between New York and New Orleans. This made

The noisy, bustling cities of the United States, with their handsome buildings and their gaslit streets, offered infinite opportunities for a young man like Al.

Al's boss angry since his boss had been trying to set up the link himself. His boss fired the clever young inventor.

Boston—The Heart of Science

Edison, now twenty-one, drifted on from job to job. In 1868, he ended up in Boston, where he took a job with the Western Union Telegraph Company. With his job safe, Edison plunged into the city's scientific life.

Boston was at the heart of everything that was happening in American science. The best technicians in the country had their workshops and businesses in Boston. And their needs were met by a variety of shops. In one of these shops, Edison bought books by Michael Faraday, the "father of electrical engineering." In other shops, like Charles Williams' electrical shop, Edison made new friends who had formed an unofficial club there. Soon he moved his lab gear into Williams' factory.

A Prank Brings Out the Inventor

Late in 1868, Edison played a prank on his Western Union bosses. To keep his speed up, he transcribed all the messages in tiny writing. The complaints from customers frustrated Edison's bosses, so they instructed him to write larger. He followed their instructions and wrote the messages in foot-high letters! Western Union was not amused. They demoted Edison, and he walked out. In January 1869, a trade journal gave the following information: "T.A. Edison has resigned his situation in the Western Union office, Boston, and will devote his time to bringing out inventions."

Risks and Failures

The young inventor soon found that his new career as an inventor was much more demanding and

Al Edison, as a young man.

The New York Stock Exchange was—and still is—at the very heart of the world's financial market.

much riskier. Unless Edison sold his inventions, he would earn nothing. He figured out a way around that problem. He would find people to put money into his projects.

While he was still at Western Union, Edison had discovered that he was a born salesman. He knew that his enthusiasm about the inventions was catching. As he explained his inventions, Edison added funny stories. Without too much of a problem, he began to find Bostonians with money.

There was one big catch—his inventions actually had to work! Some did, and some didn't. One success included a "stock ticker," a machine that businesses used to keep track of stock prices. The machine printed the information it received by wire on a long ribbon of ticker tape. Even though someone else had developed the first machine, young Edison invented an improved version, and then promptly patented it.

One of Edison's biggest failures was a duplex telegraph that could send two messages at once. Edison set up a connection between New York and Rochester, 400 miles (644 km) away on Lake Ontario. He stationed himself at Rochester. Again and again, he tried to get messages from New York, but nothing worked.

His duplex telegraph seemed useless, and its failure ruined Edison's reputation. Worse, he was out of money. It was time to be moving on again. Only eighteen months after arriving broke and hungry in Boston, young Edison moved to New York. He was still broke and hungry.

Hungry in New York

The first thing Edison needed was food. Inside a tea shop, he saw a clerk hand a customer a free sample. Young Edison marched into the shop and got a tea sample for himself. Then he bartered the tea for a meal of coffee and one apple dumpling. Feeling better, he wandered the streets in search of friends.

In New York, Edison found two friends. The first was another out-of-work telegrapher who loaned him a dollar. The second was a top telegraph engineer named Franklin L. Pope. Mr. Pope worked at New York's Gold Indicator Company, which had been founded not long before by Dr. S.S. Laws, a gold dealer and the inventor of the first version of the stock ticker.

Naturally, Mr. Pope knew of young Edison's improved version of the stock ticker. He realized Edison was just the sort of person the company needed. Pope also knew there were no job openings in the company's Wall Street headquarters in New York. But the older man had an idea. While Edison was looking for work, why didn't the

"The telegraph was still the most important application of electricity then [1860s] developed. Its value had been highlighted by the Civil War....Yet the telegraph was only an augury of things to come. In the busy workrooms of the men who made and repaired telegraph instruments there was already a burning belief that the new system could be developed, adapted, improved and expanded to carry out many tasks other than sending messages across hundreds of miles with a speed that would have been inconceivable only a generation previously.

Ronald W. Clark, from "Edison: The Man Who Made the Future"

young inventor move into the company building? Edison could sleep in the basement, use Pope's office during the day, and get to know how the transmitter on the company's ticker tape worked. Edison didn't need to be asked twice. He moved in right away.

Edison Saves Wall Street

Edison had been in the Wall Street office of the Gold Indicator Company for only a few days when chaos hit. The master ticker tape machine came to a grinding, crunching halt. It had broken down.

Within minutes, the office was full of messengers from other offices, all desperate to know what was happening. Mr. Pope and Dr. Laws were desperate as well, because Mr. Pope couldn't figure out what was wrong. Dr. Laws, who saw his business collapsing as he watched, began to shout. Mr. Pope, the engineer, and Dr. Laws, his boss, were yelling at each other when they heard someone say he could fix the broken machine.

It was young Edison. During the turmoil, Edison had noticed a broken spring that had jammed the machine's workings. Within two hours, he had the ticker tape running. By the end of the next day, he had a job helping Pope.

Edison Names His Price

At first, he worked for Dr. Laws, but later, Edison set up his own engineering business. As his reputation grew, he was hired by Western Union to sort out their equipment problems.

One day Edison's boss at Western Union called him into his office and asked the inventor how much it would cost Western Union to buy his improvements. When the inventor hesitated—he wanted $5,000 but didn't dare ask for it—the boss made an offer himself of $40,000. "This caused me

A stock ticker from the Newark factory.

to come as near fainting as I ever got," recalled Edison of the moment.

The Newark Workshop

Forty thousand dollars! It was a fortune. Edison invested the money in an empty factory in nearby Newark, New Jersey. There he set up his headquarters, creating a workshop that had space for 150 workers.

Young Edison now ran his own factory, which made stock tickers and other telegraphic equipment. And he kept inventing. He improved a newly invented system for sending telegraph messages automatically. The machine's speed was much faster than the speeds human operators could achieve. Edison also returned to work on his earlier failure—sending more than one message at a time along a single wire.

The Newark team included two men who would play an important part in the inventor's life, John Kreusi and Charles Batchelor. This close team— and a few select others who joined them—worked day and night, completely trusting their fiery "Old Man" and his convictions.

In 1871, another important person came into Edison's life. He fell in love with one of his own workers, Mary Stilwell. She was beautiful, shy, and in awe of her brilliant boss and admirer.

Edison, aged twenty-four, married Mary Stilwell on Christmas Day of 1871. Supposedly, he went straight back to his factory on his wedding day, and stayed there until midnight!

Mr. Bell's Telephone

In 1876, two things happened that had important consequences for Edison's Newark team. The first was that Edison decided to move out of town. He already had a thriving engineering works, but he

Edison's first wife, Mary.

wanted something more. He wanted to set up an "inventions factory." He envisioned this as a place that produced not just goods, but ideas. The inventor bought land in Menlo Park, a village 12 miles away from Newark. He had decided to build a laboratory there.

Another big event of the year had affected many more people than just Edison's team. In Boston, a Scotsman named Alexander Graham Bell had been working on an amazing new version of the telegraph. He was trying to use electricity to transmit the sound of the human voice, not just a message in dot-and-dash Morse code. In 1876, Bell succeeded—he had invented the telephone.

Western Union hired Edison to see if he could improve the telephone. The new invention, as amazing as it was, still needed improvements. The transmitter doubled as the receiver, so users had to juggle the equipment between mouth and ear. Its signal didn't carry for more than a few miles.

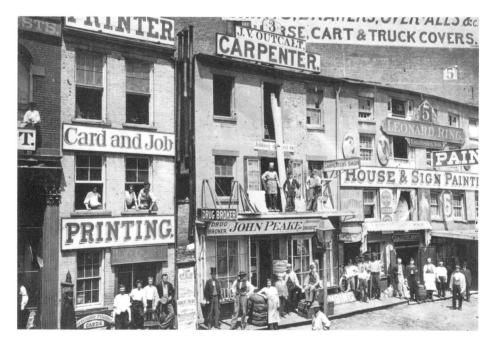

New York, as it looked in Edison's time.

Electromagnets

At the core of the telephone lay the electromagnet, an iron bar surrounded by a coil of wire. The electromagnet in the telephone was not exactly like the one used for the telegraph. Its coil was different, too, because it was not linked to a particular source of electric current. Instead, the device could, under certain conditions, produce its own electricity.

The telephone made use of a prior discovery by Michael Faraday, who knew that by activating an electromagnet, electricity could make things move. He had shown that, if the magnet in the coil moved, it started an electric current in the wire. In the telephone, the movement that started the electric current was the human voice.

Human Hearing

All the sounds humans hear are produced by vibrations from objects. As vibrations move through the air, they enter the outer ear, or auricle, and travel down the ear canal to the middle ear, or eardrum. Much like the surface of a real drum, the eardrum has a thin piece of material, called a membrane, that surrounds it. When sound waves hit the membrane, the membrane vibrates. The inner part of the ear turns these vibrations into electrical signals. The brain then translates the signals into messages that can be heard and understood.

Bell's machine, in a simple way, duplicated the human ear. When someone spoke into his telephone, the sound of the speaker's voice caused vibrations in a mechanical eardrum. This part of the telephone was a flat, thin disk of iron called a diaphragm. It was mounted inside the telephone. Next to the diaphragm was a magnet with a coil surrounding it. The movements of the vibrating disk transferred themselves to this magnet, which

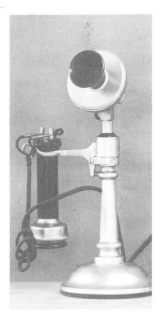

An early telephone, created by Alexander Graham Bell.

created small amounts of electric current. Because the original sounds hitting the diaphragm varied in strength and pattern, the amounts of electrical current varied, too.

The constantly varying current traveled down the wire to the telephone's receiving end. Here, the electrical variations turned themselves back into vibrations in another diaphragm. These vibrations that were the same as the original ones made by the speaker's voice. It was this voice—distorted and faint—that the listener heard.

Currents and Carbon

Edison tackled the problems of Bell's equipment one by one. First, he separated the transmitting part of the machine from the receiving part. He also developed a different method of transmission altogether. The power needed to run the telephone needed boosting as well.

For the new transmitter, Edison decided to do

without magnets completely. Instead, he planned to use the electrical principle of resistance.

Resistance hinders the flow of electricity. During his telegraphy work, he had discovered an intriguing property in carbon. When pure carbon was put under physical pressure, its resistance decreased. Edison also found that if he varied the amounts of pressure, the carbon showed varying amounts of resistance. That meant that the strength of any current flowing through the carbon would vary, too.

Edison had discovered an alternative to Bell's transmitting device. Next, he tackled the problem of needing a steady, supply of electricity.

A Battery-Powered Telephone

Edison decided that his telephone would be battery-powered. To step the power up, he used an iron bar wrapped in a double coil of wire. One of the two coiled wires led to and from the battery.

The other coiled wire, which had more turns, was connected to the telephone apparatus. When the current in the first coil was switched on and off, it triggered a powerful current in the other coil.

Night Owls

Edison still needed to perfect the transmitter. At his Menlo Park laboratory, he and his team hunted for the best way to use carbon to make a signal. Edison would start work at nightfall, break for "lunch" at midnight, and then go back to work until daybreak. Batchelor, his chief lieutenant, worked the same hours.

Edison's assistants had an easier job than he. They could hear what they were doing, and they could tell at once if something was working.

Edison shown with the Newark team. Among its members were Charles Batchelor (second from left), John Kreusi, and Colonel Gourand (seated on right).

Edison could not. Sometimes he relied on what his team said. Other times, he used his teeth to "hear." He placed the magnet that was linked to the telephone circuit between his teeth. As it vibrated, the vibrations passed through the bones of Edison's jaw and went straight to his undamaged, inner ears.

One November day in 1877, the inventor chanced to see at a shard of glass from a broken oil lamp. The glass was covered with lampblack, a powdery, black soot. This was graphite, the exact sort of carbon he needed. Edison told Charles Batchelor to make a cake of lampblack about the size of a button.

A "Splendid" Button

The moment came for the researchers to try out the lampblack. Edison's researchers placed the button of lampblack on a flat, metal plate. Gently, they positioned another plate on top of the little cake and placed the diaphragm on top of that. Then they switched on the current.

"Splendid" was how Edison later described the results of that night. The transmitter with the lampblack button had worked perfectly. The sound quality was much clearer than Bell's original telephone, and the volume was much louder. Even Edison himself could hear it!

Edison and the team had improved the telephone. Western Union paid Edison $100,000. He had produced a telephone transmitter that is basically the same as the one currently in use today.

The four weeks that followed the successful production of the telephone transmitter also brought another world-changing invention. During this one-month time period—as work on the telephone transmitter reached its climax—Edison also invented the phonograph.

Edison in later life, using the telephone that he helped to perfect.

Off and on, Edison had been working on the phonograph for months. He loved having several projects going on at the same time. That way, he reasoned, if he got stuck on one invention, he'd turn to another. Usually, a solution to at least one invention would pop into his head.

A Talking Toy

During the summer of 1877, Edison made a toy for his five-year-old daughter, Marion. It was a model of a man sawing wood who had an odd-looking funnel on the top of its head. Marion asked her father what the funnel was for.

Edison loudly recited a rhyme into the funnel. The little model not only started sawing wood but also started to talk! When Edison shouted into the toy's

Left: *Electric light bulbs of Edison's own design still light the big laboratory on the upper floor of Menlo Park's main building.*

Opposite: *Edison created a "speaking" doll for his daughter, Marion, several months before he invented the phonograph.*

funnel-shaped mouthpiece, the diaphragm's vibrations had set the machinery in motion.

A Recording of the Human Voice

The phonograph took the idea from Marion's toy several stages further. Edison had noticed that, if he shouted at a diaphragm with a pin mounted on it, he could make marks on a piece of coated paper. He also noticed that, if the paper was pulled under the pin again, it made a sound that somewhat resembled words.

But in both the United States and France, other scientists had begun to work on the idea of turning the vibrations of the human voice into marks on a hard surface. In November, Edison knew he would have to act quickly on his idea. By December 4, he

"My plan was to synchronize the camera and the phonograph so as to record sounds when the pictures were made, and reproduce the two in harmony....We did a lot of work along this line, and my talking pictures were shown in many theaters in the United States and foreign countries....We had the first of the so-called 'Talking Pictures' in our laboratory thirty years ago."

Edison, recalling the birth of the Kinetoscope in 1925

had given John Kreusi some puzzling directions. He told his colleague to build a machine that contained a grooved cylinder, flanked by twin diaphragms and needles. By December 6, the machine was ready. The nursery rhyme, "Mary Had a Little Lamb," was about to become the first recording of the human voice.

The Needle in the Furrow

The processes for how the phonograph worked was quite simple. Edison's voice, as it recited the rhyme, made the recording diaphragm vibrate. A needle under the diaphragm cut a groove in the brass of a tinfoil-covered cylinder that also turned as the diaphragm vibrated. As the diaphragm moved in and out, the needle pressed harder or more gently on the tinfoil moving underneath it.

This 1878 cartoon, from the British magazine, Punch, *pokes fun at Edison's powers of invention by illustrating anti-gravity underwear!*

EDISON'S ANTI–GRAVITATION UNDER–CLOTHING
Tommy. „Oh! Don't wind us in yet, Mamma! It's so jolly up here, and not a bit cold!"

The sounds of the nursery rhyme were translated as varying depths in the groove that the needle cut in the tinfoil. To translate them back, they just needed to be transferred again to the diaphragm, which had its own needle.

The Wizard of Menlo Park

The talking machine caused an instant sensation. Its inventor, in the habit of thinking like a newspaper reporter, took the phonograph to the office of the journal, *Scientific American*, and played the recording of "Mary Had a Little Lamb" to the editor and his staff. At first, the audience was stunned and silent. Then they went wild with enthusiasm.

The rest of the world joined in. The French called him "this astonishing Edison." The British hailed him as a great discoverer. In the United States, President Hayes demanded that he hear the new invention at the White House. Ordinary Americans turned Thomas Edison into a hero. From then on Edison was, in their words, "The Wizard of Menlo Park."

Creating Light

It was 1879—less than two years after Edison had made his great breakthroughs in sound technology. Edison and Batchelor walked the short space between Menlo Park's main laboratory to the glass blower's shed directly behind the building. Charles Batchelor carried something in his hands.

The two men entered the shed very carefully. They paced across to a workbench—and stopped. Edison cursed. Batchelor stared down at what he held: two pieces of wire and two slender lengths of hard, dark material, curved like a horseshoe. The horseshoe-shaped wire had broken.

The pair trudged back to the lab. On one of the tables there, among all the scientific clutter, lay a

reel of sewing thread. Edison cut off a small piece of thread. Carefully, he fastened each end of the tiny thread to a piece of platinum wire. Then he coaxed it into a groove cut inside a metal block. Covering it with another piece of metal, he slid the metal block into a furnace.

Making the Electric Lightbulb

There was a long wait. Batchelor slumped in a chair, and Edison caught up on some much-needed sleep. Both men were exhausted.

Late in the afternoon, the cotton in its metal case was ready. The two men opened the case and gently took out the delicate horseshoe-shaped carbon filament that the thread had become. Then they enclosed it in a glass globe. Next, they pumped out all the air from the globe so that the carbon filament would be in a vacuum.

If Edison's plans worked out, a current flowing through the carbonized cotton would make his

Opposite: *An Edison lightbulb.*

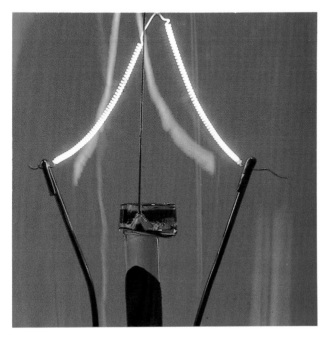

A tungsten filament in this modern lightbulb heats up when an electric current passes through it.

glass globe glow with a clear, steady light. In light bulbs other inventors were trying to make, the fil- ament burned out within a few minutes. Edison felt that a carbonized cotton filament was different. And, in the vacuum of the glass globe, the light would last.

Edison and Batchelor felt that this time they would be successful. But, in one careless move- ment, a screwdriver tumbled from its place on the crowded bench and fell against the fragile, carbon horseshoe. Once again, the carbon broke.

Numb from exhaustion, the two men repeated the time-consuming procedure: cotton wires, metal case, furnace. Then they waited. At last, the third carbon of the day was ready. Edison and his com- panion freed it from its case, and carried it across the yard. They enclosed it in the safety of a waiting glass globe. The pump was set to work. Little by little, all but the tiniest amount of air was driven out of the globe. By 1:30 A.M., the globe was ready.

The Light That Lasted

As his laboratory workers watched, Edison turned on the electric current. And there, like a tawny star- burst, was the light! Everyone gasped and held their breath. Then, as the light stayed on, everyone seemed to breathe normally again. The light was still on an hour later. Two hours later, it still shone. Three hours later, the glow was still steady.

Dawn came with its promise of another hot, dry October day. The glow of the carbon filament faded in the daylight, but it continued to burn. With all fatigue forgotten, Edison and his team watched the glow with great satisfaction and joy. By 3 P.M., when the glass on the lamp finally cracked, the filament had been burning for over thirteen hours!

That Christmas, the "Wizard of Menlo Park" lit

up his home and laboratory with dozens of his new lights. In the midwinter darkness, lamps lined the roads and glowed in the windows of Menlo Park. Thousands of visitors from all over the United States came to see the vision of light, jostling each other and exclaiming with excitement. This was only the start, Edison told them. He planned to light up New York City itself.

A Rival to Gaslight

Edison's initial interest in electric light went back even further than his triumphs with sound. But he had only started to pay attention to it in 1878 when, after a year of frenzied work, he felt he needed a change. From the beginning, Edison had a clear idea of what he wanted to achieve. He wanted to develop something that would rival the United States' multi-million dollar gas industry. Because the gas industry had no competition, the gas companies often did just as they pleased—with no regard for the law or for people's rights. Their dominance had been causing a growing resentment in the general public. Edison's intent in developing electricity was to put the gas industry out of business.

Gas made from coal had been in use since early in the nineteenth century. It was distributed to customers by underground pipes. People lit their homes with gas and used more primitive oil lamps.

Edison's goal was nothing less than the creation of a completely new power system. The way he was planning it, homes that used electric lighting would be linked to a central power station, just as they already were to gas plants. And the link would not be made with pipes, but with shining, copper wire; Edison planned to install miles of copper wire, which would hold a whole city together, much like a web.

Today, oil lamps like these are regarded as antiques. For the people of Edison's time, they were a vital part of everyday life.

This scene shows a gaslit section of London in the nineteenth century.

The First Priority

The arc light, the type that was used before Edison's electric light, was invented in Britain by Sir Humphry Davy in 1812. An alternative to gas, arc lights used electric current that jumped across a gap between two pieces of carbon. Its use was restricted to streetlighting mostly because the lights glared, and they produced both smoke and a strong smell. All arc lights were wired in a series or in a pattern that resembled the beads on a necklace. As the current flowed through the wire, it passed through every single arc light. It was not possible to turn off a single light by itself. The whole series had to be turned off and on together.

Edison's first priority for introducing electric lights was clear. He had to get electricity to all the lamps owned by large numbers of individual subscribers. And each of these individual subscribers had to be able to turn any single lamp on and off at any moment. Edison knew that this meant that the lamps had to be wired in a special way—a way few people had tried. Electrical wiring has to take the form of a closed loop, or circuit, which leads back and forth from a power source. The loop goes out from a power source and then back to it, looking much like a necklace. The wiring pattern Edison decided to use instead was called a parallel circuit. The wiring diagram for this type of circuit looked more like a ladder. On each of the ladder's rungs was a light. The current flowed down one of the ladder's uprights and back up the other. It also flowed across the rungs, feeding the light as long as the lights were turned on. If a light was turned off, the current "missed" that rung, and continued on its way around the rest of the circuit.

Gas was first used for lighting in the late eighteenth century. This footed lamplighter, wearing an eighteenth-century costume, needed the ladder to climb up to each lamp.

Ohm's Law

The first plans Edison drew up that used parallel circuits had an excessive amount of copper wire. Setting up such a system would have bankrupted anyone who tried it. Edison knew he needed to figure out a way to reduce the costs.

Edison had often boasted that he didn't understand one of the basic laws of electricity, named after Georg Ohm, the German scientist. But Edison used Ohm's Law to solve the problem that faced him. Ohm's Law helps people to set up the mathematics principles that are needed to create an electrical circuit. The law says there is a connection between the strength of a current, the amount of resistance in the substance it flows through, and the force that makes the current flow. This force—the "push" behind the current—is measured in units called volts. The units describing a current's strength are called amperes.

Resistance is measured in units called ohms, named after Ohm himself. Ohm's Law says that the size of the current depends on the amount of force behind it, divided by the amount of resistance involved.

Cost Cutting

To cut his copper costs, Edison knew he had to cut the size of the current he used. But parallel circuits usually needed a strong current. He wondered if could make a weaker current that could do the same job. Ohm's Law provided the answer. Edison would build more resistance into the circuit. First he experimented with carbon, but it burned out before the right temperature was reached. Edison then tried platinum, but it melted when it was heated to the right temperature. Then he discovered how to get a very high vacuum in his light bulbs by using a Sprengel pump.

The very high vacuum meant that more air—and therefore more oxygen—had been removed from inside the bulb. This prevented the filament from burning out too quickly. The cotton carbon filament, combined with an effective vacuum, meant that Edison knew he could distribute electric power at a reasonable price.

"Long-Waisted Mary Ann"

By the time he had perfected the problems with the bulb itself, Edison had also figured out how to produce the electricity his new system would need. He would use a generator, or dynamo. It was a machine that used Faraday's discovery about converting movement into electricity. Edison's dynamo turned steam power into electric power. To make his calculations work, the dynamo had to produce a current of a constant voltage. At the time, all dynamos were extremely inefficient. Edison set about designing his own, more efficient dynamo.

Opposite: Edison takes a catnap on a laboratory bench.

Below: Holborn Viaduct, one of the first London streets to be lit by electricity.

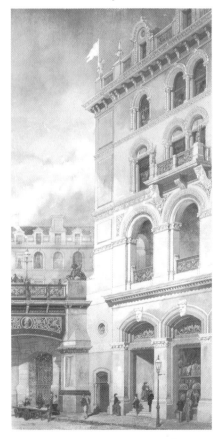

In the summer of 1879, he and his team succeeded in building the first truly energy-efficient dynamo. The machine Edison and his team built looked like nothing engineers had ever seen before. Edison's workers coined a nickname for the towering monster they'd made. She became the "Long-waisted Mary Ann."

All Aboard!

Linked to a steam engine in an adjacent room, the "Mary Ann" was brilliantly efficient. She converted steam into electricity with a loss of no more than one-fifth of the energy involved.

Edison soon worked out an extra way to use his new machine. In 1880, the inventor used it to drive the United States' first full-sized electric train. The year before, the German company, Siemans, had demonstrated a similar train at the Berlin Trade Fair. The "Wizard of Menlo Park"

"He could go to sleep anywhere, any time, on anything. I have seen him asleep on a work bench with his arm for a pillow; in a chair with his feet on his desk; on a cot with all his clothes on. I have seen him sleep for thirty-six hours at a stretch, interrupted for only an hour while he consumed a large steak, potatoes and pie, and smoked a cigar, and I have known him to go to sleep standing on his feet."

Thomas Edison remembered by his colleague Alfred O. Tate

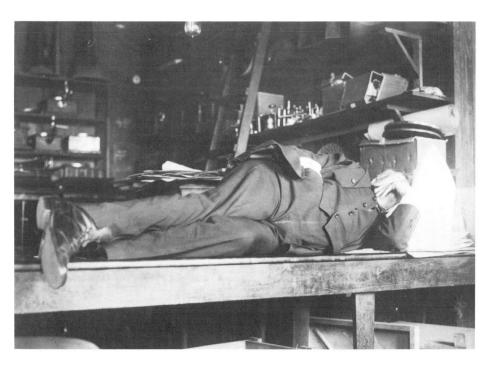

decided to test his own. He had metal rails laid around the Menlo Park grounds and converted a "Mary Ann" dynamo into an electric motor.

On May 13, all was ready. Edison ordered the power to be switched on. He climbed aboard the train. Visitors and staff followed, packing themselves into the little carriage wherever they could. Batchelor, who was sitting on a crate that was the driver's seat, switched on the engine. Off they went, bouncing, jouncing, and clinging on for their lives as the train rattled around curves at 25 miles (40 km) an hour. The return journey was less exciting. The engine broke down, and the passengers had to get out and push!

The railway was another success for Edison. In September 1881, the Electric Railway Company of America was founded. But Edison soon vanished back into the complex world of electric light, and the company failed to prosper.

Will the Lamps Light?

It was 2:45 P.M. on the afternoon of September 4, 1882. In grimy New York City, people sweated in the heat. Throughout the building at 255 Pearl Street, anxiety abounded. In the nearby financial district, tension also filled the Wall Street offices of J. P. Morgan, the great banker.

The directors of the Edison Electric Light Company kept taking out their watches, looking at them, and pocketing them again. Looking around the room, they eyed the waiting lights, with their shining glass globes. Then they eyed Edison, who paced nervously. Underground wires connected the lights to the Pearl Street building, which housed Edison's electric lighting scheme. At the heart of Edison's plan for lighting up the world was the power station that would supply electricity to the electricity company's subscribers. At 3:00 P.M.,

Opposite top:

Edison's second laboratory at West Orange, New Jersey.

Opposite bottom:

The chemistry lab in the "inventions factory."

By 1890, this Edison power station, with its giant dynamos, work-shops, and offices, was supplying subscribers in Brooklyn, across the East River, from the original Pearl Street station. Only eight years before, when the Pearl Street station opened, it had—in Edison's own words—"no parallel in the world."

the great generator at Pearl Street would be set in action. In offices and other buildings around the area, 400 "Edison lamps" would come on. The tension was created by not knowing whether they would come on or not.

Edison Waits

Edison continued to pace the Wall Street office floor. Events of the past four years whirled around in his head. He thought about everything—the false starts, the struggles, and the triumphs. He also remembered the moments of horror when—in July—the Pearl Street generators had run amok. There had also been fights about money, fights with the threatened gas companies, and fights with other scientists who didn't believe Edison could accomplish what he set out to do. It was a tension and struggle he had faced constantly as he had developed the electric lighting system.

Abruptly, the inventor's thoughts darted back to the generator. For safety, the power station was only using one. He questioned whether it would work or not. He knew it could possibly run amok again. If that happened he wondered if the workers would know what to do. None of them had any prior experience in running a central power station. Edison, the "wizard"—usually so bold and confident—was, for once, afraid.

On all the clocks and watches, the hour hand slowly dragged round to three. Everyone was watching the Edison lamps. Time—at least for a second—seemed to stand still.

Then, inside the glass globes, a tiny curl of light shaped like a horseshoe appeared. Swiftly, the glow gathered strength and then shone out brightly. The work of dozens of dedicated scientists who had worked on electricity over decades had been worthwhile. Edison's great gamble had succeeded. It was 3 P.M., and the Age of Electricity had begun.

By evening, Edison's lights gleamed across lower New York in offices as well as homes, all giving out their soft, radiant light. Edison, meanwhile, was no longer the neatly dressed person who had paced back and forth. With collar gone, and his white felt hat smudged, he had returned to his usual look. In fact, he had spent part of the afternoon down a street manhole, hunting for a fuse that had blown.

Mission Accomplished

After the lights came on that September afternoon, Edison told reporters, "I have accomplished all that I promised." Unlike many of his statements to the press, Edison did not consider this one boasting. To him, it was the truth. Turning on the electricity at Pearl Street marked the pinnacle of his many

"The Pearl Street station was the biggest and most responsible thing I had ever undertaken. It was a gigantic problem, with many ramifications....Success meant world-wide adoption of our central-station plan. Failure meant loss of money and prestige and setting back of our enterprise. All I can remember of the events of that day is that I had been up most of the night rehearsing my men and going over every part of the system....If I ever did any thinking in my life it was on that day."

Thomas Edison, recalling September 4, 1882

The now-famous lights of New York began at Pearl Street in 1882.

achievements. The Edison who had created the new energy system on Pearl Street was now a famous engineer and business person. The new energy system took time to catch on. But, in the meantime, Edison became famous again—for the phonograph.

New Frontiers

By the end of the 1880s, Edison's life had changed dramatically. His success with the phonograph and the lightbulb had made him a very rich man. Edison left his Menlo Park base and was in the process of building a new one in West Orange, New Jersey. He also had a new wife.

His first wife, Mary, had died in 1884 from typhoid fever. Two years later, Edison, now aged thirty-nine, had married a beautiful, sophisticated woman named Mina Miller. Mina, who came from a wealthy family, hoped to house-train her tobacco-chewing, work-obsessed husband. Throughout their lives together, she always tried to make her world-famous inventor husband behave in a way that fitted his wealth and status. Much as Edison loved her, Mina seldom succeeded!

Improving the Phonograph

In 1887, for the second time in his life, Edison found himself jolted into a new project by the work of Alexander Graham Bell. Bell had also produced a phonograph, but he recognized Edison's important contributions to its development. Bell suggested to Edison that they join forces and market the new machine under both of their names.

Edison was enraged. He decided to resurrect the machine he had built ten years before rather than allow anyone to share the credit of the invention. Edison worked nonstop on it for a year. He got rid of the fragile tinfoil that had surrounded the cylinder. Instead, he developed a wax cylinder with a sapphire for a needle and a more sophisticated pick-up head, Edison's revised phonograph machine worked much better.

By now, Edison was quite deaf. He struggled to improve the machine, reverting to his old method of sound testing by biting the machine's amplifying equipment. That way he hoped to feel the sounds that could not penetrate his ears.

The Entertainment Machine

Edison had always viewed the primary use of the phonograph as way for business people to dictate letters.

Edison's second wife, Mina.

....

"He invents all the while, even in his dreams."

Mina Edison,
describing her husband

....

In this carefully posed photograph, taken in 1888, and later used as an advertisement, Edison slumps beside his improved version of the phonograph.

But the public thought differently. Instead, they were charmed by the magic machine that reproduced the sounds of a choir or an orchestra. Children loved Edison's talking dolls. And people flocked to push coins into an early version of the juke-box, which was called the nickelodeon.

Whatever Edison may have planned or intended, the "sound-writer" became a major force in American entertainment. Even though the phonograph was eventually replaced by Emile Berliner's gramophone, Edison is credited as the person who gave sound recordings to the world.

Moving Pictures

With scarcely a pause, Edison added moving pictures to his sound recordings. By the 1880s, others had attempted to produce pictures that moved. The earliest of these "moving" pictures were drawings. Each picture showed one tiny stage of motion, such as a horse trotting. If the series of pictures were viewed in a quick sequence, the viewer would see a blurry, trotting horse, for example.

By Edison's time, a British photographer, Eadweard Muybridge, was making "moving pictures" with photographs. Each one was taken by a different still camera that used glass photographic plates. But one minute of film of a trotting horse needed over 700 cameras to shoot it! Muybridge met Edison in 1888, and they discussed making phonograph records to go with photographs. The idea was dropped because Muybridge didn't think the phonograph would be loud enough to use with a large audience.

Muybridge's visit had given Edison an idea.

Edison, who was working on his phonograph at the same time, had cylinders on his mind. He decided to coat one with a light-sensitive material and place it inside his camera. As each picture was taken, the cylinder rotated slightly. When the "film" was developed, the cylinder contained a spiral, or band of little photographs running around it. The viewer supplied the motion by turning the cylinder. Edison coined a name for his new invention by using part of the word *kinetics*, meaning the science of motion. He called his invention the "kinetoscope."

In Britain, another photographer, William Friese-Greene, was experimenting with celluloid film, invented by the American, George Eastman. In 1889, Edison obtained some of the Eastman celluloid film himself that had been made into long strips at his request. Very soon, Mr. Edison had built a camera that would feed the long strips through at a steady rate. To view the developed film, Edison then invented an individual viewer. At the same time, he considered projecting the film onto large screens, but he eventually rejected the idea as too costly. In the meantime, he had a movie studio built at West Orange, where he made films of boxers, dancers, and circus acts. He patented the idea for motion pictures, but he did not extend the patent outside the United States. He also forgot to mention the idea of projection in his patent.

In 1894, a Frenchman named Lumiere bought an Edison kinetoscope and gave it to his sons. The Lumieres quickly adapted the Edison kinetoscope to work with a projector. In 1895, Mr. Lumiere and his sons opened the world's first public cinema. They were the first people to bring cinema to large-scale audiences, using an Edison kinetoscope as the basis of their system.

The Grand Old Man of Science

In 1891, when Edison was forty-four, he applied for a patent on the kinetoscope. He was almost exactly halfway through his life. During the next

Frames from "The Sneeze," one of the first movies ever made. The star was John Ott, a member of Edison's team. The movie had its own sound effects that were recorded on the phonograph.

53

forty years, his reputation grew and grew. Already one of the most famous living Americans, Edison was the grand old man of science, a friend to presidents, and a friend to great industrialists like Henry Ford. Despite all his fame and considerable influence, he was still plain, wise-cracking Al Edison, the man who chewed tobacco and told funny stories. To young children growing up, Thomas Edison was nothing short of an all-American hero.

Losing a Fortune

By the late 1880s, Mr. Edison's "magic touch" slowly began to fade. He still had all sorts of ideas and schemes, but his triumphs became rarer.

In one scheme during the 1890s, for instance, he lost a fortune on a project to extract iron from the low-grade ore deposits. He even built his own mine in New Jersey and then invented the machinery he needed to work the mine. By the worst of luck, at almost the same time, high-grade ore deposits were discovered elsewhere that could be mined more cheaply. The price of iron plummeted, and Edison's project failed, taking $2 million with it. "Well, it's all gone, but we had...a good time spending it," said Edison soon after the loss.

Edison later used his mining expertise to set up a cement works. And, in a short while, he had revolutionized the way cement was made. Edison experimented with making concrete roads and even concrete houses.

Although the road-making project was a failure, it was linked to something else that came much closer to success. Edison's exploration of concrete and road-making eventually led to the production of an electric car.

It was the automobile that forged his friendship with Henry Ford. The two men first met in 1896,

"Visions of the Year 2000", drawn at the very end of the nineteenth century: an electrical floor-cleaner, and the audio-newspaper, and a dictating machine. The electric cleaner and dictaphone came directly from Edison's work. Although Edison did not invent radio equipment, his experiments helped the inventor of the radio valve and electron tube, Ambrose Fleming.

Fast friends, Henry Ford and Al Edison take a ride in one of Ford's own cars.

the year Ford brought out his first car. Ford deeply admired Edison, and the two got on brilliantly. Edison applauded Ford's gasoline-fueled vehicle. On his own, Edison began to work on a battery-driven car instead.

For ten years, Edison worked to produce a storage battery that would keep a car going for a hundred miles with a cruising speed of 25 mph (40 km). The attempt cost him a million dollars. In 1909, when Edison was satisfied with the results of his storage battery, he decided that the car was ready to be sold. Some firms had even brought out electric cars and trucks that used it. But, once again—just like the iron-works—the great inventor was unlucky with his timing.

No Giving Up

The year before, Ford had produced the famous "Tin Lizzie." This was a cheap, gasoline-fueled Model T, which brought the price of a car within the reach of ordinary families. From then on, the link between the car and the gasoline engine was unbreakable. Edison had come on the scene too late.

Characteristically, Edison did not give up. By 1912, at Ford's request, Edison applied his hard-earned knowledge to designing a battery-powered self starter for the Model T itself. He struggled with this task and worked sixteen hours a day in the 1920s, when he was over seventy. At that time, a happy ending to the saga of the storage batteries unexpectedly appeared. The batteries were success-ful for other purposes, and they were making money. In making a profit, the batteries fulfilled Edison's prime goal, worked out so many years before—to invent things that would sell.

The Lights Dim

On the night of October 18, 1931, Edison died, aged eighty-four. He died from a combination of diabetes, kidney disease, a gastric ulcer, and a life-time of hard work that took a toll on his body. On the day of his funeral, it was proposed that the nation should mourn Edison by turning the elec-tricity off. Though it would have been a fitting tribute, Americans soon realized it couldn't be done. The United States, without electricity, would have meant disaster. In factories, machinery would halt and electric trains would stop running. Oil wells would stop pumping. In the city's high-rise buildings, people would be stranded halfway to the sky because the elevators would stop, too. And what about hospitals that relied on electricity? And offices? And the growing number of farms?

Plans were quickly changed. President Hoover proposed that mourners should turn off any lights that were not essential. Americans everywhere agreed. On the evening of October 21, 1931, a great shadow, like an eclipse, swept across the

"An inventor frequently wastes his time and his money trying to extend his invention to uses for which it is not at all suit-able. Edison has never done this. He rides no hobbies. He views each problem that comes up as a thing of itself, to be solved in exactly the right way....His knowl-edge is so nearly univer-sal that he cannot be classified as a electrician or a chemist—in fact, Mr. Edison cannot be classi-fied. The more I have seen of him the greater he has appeared to me—both as a servant of humanity and as a man."

Henry Ford

Magnified many times, the diamond stylus of a record player rests lightly in the spiral groove of a record.

country. Even the Statute of Liberty briefly held a darkened torch.

The Legacy of a Creative Genius

The debate over Thomas Alva Edison's memorial shows what he left behind. Some inventors who have changed the world did do so with just one invention. Edison, in contrast, could number his creations in dozens, even in hundreds. Edison invented because he could not help himself. The list of what Mr. Edison achieved is staggering in both its length and complexity. In all, he took out 1,093 patents on his work.

For each famous achievement, such as the phonograph and electric light, there are several, less well-known inventions that were forerunners of machines we know and use today. The phonograph doubled as a dictaphone, and was also the

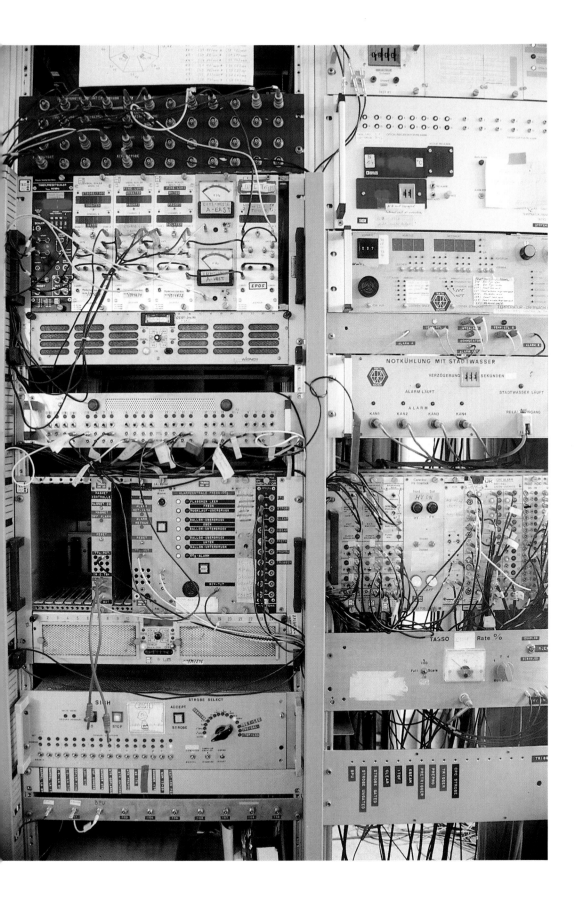

first answering machine. His prefabricated houses found an echo in later building methods.

Most important of all, there was his "Edison-effect" lamp, from which the foundations of the science of electronics grew. Although Edison was intrigued by the mysteries of the "effect," the overworked inventor did not follow up on its implications. In the early 1900s, Ambrose Fleming, a British engineer, used Edison's "Edison-effect" lamp to create the electronic radio valve.

Thanks, Mr. Wizard

Throughout his life, Edison's rivals continually accused him of stealing their glory. He accused them back. Many scientists, in fact, were working simultaneously on similar projects, so it is extremely hard to determine who really did what first. Regardless of the disputes, it is obvious that the world would have been much a different place if Edison had never lived or invented.

It would be wrong to say that, without Edison, we would still be living with gas lamps, open fires, or steam-powered sewing machines. At some point, someone would probably have eventually designed a power system as effective as Edison's. Someone, too, would probably have turned Bell's telephone into a practical machine. But it is less likely that someone would have invented the phonograph, which owed almost nothing to any other earlier work.

The truth is that we can never know what our lives would have been like if Edison, the "Wizard of Menlo Park," had never invented anything. His nickname was apt. The power of the Wizard was Edison's ability to transform the everyday into something new. Edison transformed tinfoil into sound and cotton thread into light. Thomas Alva Edison and his genius transformed everyday life.

. . . .

"One day, we may harness the rise and fall of the tides and imprison the rays of the sun."

Thomas Edison, in 1922

. . . .

Important Dates

1847	February 11: Thomas Alva Edison is born in Milan, Ohio.
1854	The Edison family moves to Port Huron, Michigan. Soon after this, Edison catches scarlet fever, and is seriously ill. This illness may have been the initial cause of his later deafness.
1855	Edison spends three months in the school of the Rev. G.B. Engle.
1859	Edison, aged twelve, becomes a newsboy on the Detroit-Port Huron railway line.
1861	The Civil War breaks out between the anti-slavery northern states and the southern ones with their slave-based economy.
1863	Edison becomes a telegrapher at sixteen and spends the next few years wandering from one telegraph job to another.
1868	Edison arrives in Boston and takes a job at the Western Union Telegraph Company. He applies for his first patent (on the vote-recorder), and news of his duplex apparatus is written up in the telegraphers' trade journal.
1869	January: Edison sets up on his own as a freelance inventor. He applies for his second patent, on improvements to the stock ticker. April: Trials of his duplex apparatus fail. October: Edison and Franklin L. Pope set up in partnership as electrical engineers.
1871	Edison establishes his manufacturing shop in Newark, New Jersey. December: Thomas Edison marries Mary Stilwell.
1874	Edison successfully produces a new multi-message telegraph system, the quadruplex, which can send two messages from each end of the wire at the same time.
1876	January: Edison starts to set up a new laboratory, in Menlo Park, New Jersey, and moves in later in the year. March: Alexander Graham Bell is granted a patent for his newly invented telephone.
1877	January: Edison begins work on his carbon telephone transmitter. November: Edison uses a lampblack "button" to make huge improvements in his carbon transmitter's effectiveness.
1878	Edison starts work on the electric light and a system for distributing electricity.
1879	Summer: Edison designs the "Long-Waisted Mary Ann."
1879	October: Edison discovers that a filament of carbonized cotton thread, placed in a high vacuum inside a glass globe, will give out many hours of light before burning out.
1880	Edison builds an electric railway in Menlo Park.

1881	Edison leaves Menlo Park and moves back to New York.
1882	While working on the electric light, Edison notices a black deposit on the inside of the lightbulb, the first evidence of the "Edison effect."
1884	Edison's wife, Mary, dies.
1886	Thomas Edison marries Mina Miller, and settles with her at "Glenmont," a big estate in the Orange Valley, New Jersey.
1887	Edison starts work on improving the phonograph; he also builds a large new laboratory at West Orange.
1888	Edison revives an iron-ore processing company started in the 1870s. Over the following years, he buys land in New Jersey with iron deposits, and sets up an ore-processing plant and a mining village.
1891	Edison patents his kinetoscope in the United States.
1899	Edison begins work on developing a battery for electric cars.
1900	Edison's work on iron-ore processing is finally dropped.
1902	Edison sets up a successful cement works. His road-making and house-building projects develop from this business.
1912	Edison starts work on designing an electric self-starter for Henry Ford's Model T, which has ousted electric cars from the market.
1914-1918	World War I. Edison spends much time working on scientific developments for the United States Navy.
1927	Edison sets up a laboratory in Florida to research home-grown sources of rubber, as an alternative to the usual Malayan product.
1931	August: Edison collapses, and is diagnosed as dangerously ill. October 18: Thomas Alva Edison dies, aged eighty-four. October 21: The United States turns off its lights in mourning.

For More Information

Books

Dineen, Jacqueline. *The Early Inventions* (Ideas That Changed the World) New York, NY: Chelsea House, 1995.

Nirgiotis, Nicholas. *Thomas Edison* (Cornerstones of Freedom). Danbury, CT: Children's Press, 1994.

Parker, Steve. *Thomas Edison and Electricity* (Science Discoveries). New York, NY; Chelsea House, 1995.

Web Site

Thomas Edison and Menlo Park

Learn more about this famous scientist, his childhood, Menlo Park Laboratory, and the hundreds of inventions and patents he produced— www.hfmgv.org/histories/edison/tae.html

Glossary

Ampere: The unit used for measuring the rate of flow of an electric current or its size (strength). It is named after André Ampére, who researched electromagnetism in the 1820s.

Battery: A source of electricity which works, not by converting movement into electricity, but by chemical reaction. The first battery, made by the Italian scientist Alessandro Volta, was made up of silver, zinc, and wet cardboard, which reacted on each other to produce an electric current.

Circuit: The closed-loop pattern used for electrical wiring. Circuits lead both from and back to the power source, passing through one or more electric appliances on the way.

Diaphragm: A thin, springy piece of material, often metal, which vibrates easily.

Duplex: A telegraphic system for sending two messages over the same wire. In the 1870s, Edison successfully developed a refinement, the "quadru-plex", that sent four messages over the same wire—two from each end.

Dynamo: A machine that converts movement into electricity, using magnetic induction—is often called a generator. One well-known type of dynamo is the appliance that converts the movement of a cyclist's feet into electricity to light a bicycle lamp.

Edison effect: Edison's discovery of an electric current flowing from one leg of a light filament across the vacuum inside a light bulb, without wires to carry it. This finding, which pointed the way to the science of electronics, would later be of crucial importance to other scientists.

Electromagnet: A "temporary" magnet made out of a piece (or "core") of iron wrapped in a coil of wire linked to an electric power source. When the current is turned on, the iron becomes a magnet. The first electromagnet was made by an Englishman named William Sturgeon in 1824.

Filament: The threadlike fitting inside a lightbulb which, when the current is turned on, heats up and glows. Edison's first successful filament was made out of carbonized sewing thread. Later, he used carbonized bamboo. Modern filaments are made of metal.

Induction, electromagnetic: The generation of electrical energy through movement, by changing the relative positions of a magnet and a coil of wire. This way of generating electricity was discovered by the scientist Michael Faraday in 1831.

Kinetoscope: The peepshow-type apparatus invented by Edison for viewing films made with his "kinetographic" (moving-picture) camera. "Kineto" comes from a Greek word for movement.

Membrane: A thin, stretchy piece of tissue, often skin.

Morse code: The communication system invented by American artist Samuel Morse in the 1830s, for use with the telegraph system he was developing. It consists of a mixture of short and long signals ("dots" and "dashes"). Each letter of the alphabet is assigned its own code value.

Ohm: The unit used for measuring electrical resistance. It is named after the German scientist Georg Ohm, who studies the links between current, resistance, and voltage in the 1820s.

Phonograph: The machine for recording and playing back sounds, invented by Edison in 1877, and later developed into the (disc-playing) gramophone.

Resistance: The degree to which a substance impedes the flow of an electric current.

Semaphore: A line-of-sight system of communication, in which coded signals are sent either by mechanical apparatus or by holding flag (or the arms) in different positions. It was invented in the 1790s.

Telegraph: A long-distance communications system (and its apparatus) involving the transmission of electrical signals in Morse code along wires connecting sender and receiver. It was developed over the 1830s and 1840s and it sometimes called "electric" to distinguish it from the earlier semaphore apparatus, which was also called the telegraph.

Volt: The unit, named after Alessandro Volta, used to measure electrical force or the degree of pressure "pushing" an electric current around a circuit.

Index